What Time Is It?

one o'clock

two o'clock

three o'clock

four o'clock

five o'clock

six o'clock

seven o'clock

eight o'clock

What time is it?

It's one o'clock.

What time is it?

It's two o'clock.

What time is it?

It's three o'clock.

What time is it?

It's four o'clock.

What time is it?

It's five o'clock.

What time is it?

It's six o'clock.

Let's learn more about France.

Croissant